I0111315

All Scripture references taken from the KJV of the Holy Bible, unless otherwise indicated.

I AM NOT YOUR TARGET: Warfare Prayers Against Haters & the Powers They Employ, by Dr. Marlene Miles

Freshwater Press 2025

Freshwaterpress9@gmail.com

ISBN: 978-1-967860-20-3

Paperback Version

Table of Contents

I AM NOT YOUR TARGET

Warfare Against Haters & the Powers They Employ

Freshwater

Introduction

This book is chiefly a prayerbook. The prayer points will be enumerated in the print versions only. The digital version does not support the enumeration of the prayer points. But in print the numbers are there for ease of following and praying if praying with another or others. The Scriptures are to be prayed, but they are not enumerated because the Chapter and Verse designations are more important than adding another number adjacent to those verses. The sections are divided to make things more manageable, more readable, or more easily prayed. but they were not there in the original prayer, which can be found on Warfare Prayer Channel.

By being targeted,, in this book it means a concerted effort to do something nefarious or evil to another person by spiritual means that the hater believes will remain hidden to the intended person who is their target. The impetus for it is most often jealousy, hatred, or covetousness. By being targeted we gain the inference that someone is in someone else's sights and may be shot at or fired upon, this will mean most often, spiritually in this book. It could mean in the natural as well because if Cain had had a gun...

If I have sinned, what have I done to You, Watcher of mankind? Why have You made me Your target, so that I have become a burden to You? (Job 7:20, HCSB, ISV, NASB, NET, LEB).

We know that Job is the oldest Book in the Bible, and we also know that Job thought that all the stuff he was going through was God directly punishing him, not knowing there was a punisher--, the devil. This verse though, let's us know that Job did get something right, that he was a target and that he was being shot at. Then thousands of years later and with the Holy Spirit shall we not also realize when we have been made a target for assaults, insults and evil arrows, or worse?

I was at ease, but He shattered me; He seized me by the scruff of the neck and smashed me to pieces. He set me up as His target; (Job 16:12 HCSB, ISV, NASB, NET, AM, LEB, WEB)

Yes, Job was a target, but it was not God that had targeted him. We know that the Accuser of the Brethren had gone to God to ask for permission to test Job in this way. As the Accuser accuses man to God, day and night we should do well to walk circumspectly so that there is no reproach against us. However, iniquity is the magnet that attracts these accusations and sometimes that iniquity is inherited through bloodlines.

1. Lord, in the Name of Jesus, blot out and forget the iniquity of my fore parents, remember it no more, in the Name of Jesus.

God will hear our prayers and our requests, but if the iniquity hasn't been inherited, but is fresh and brand new because of what you did, then you must repent daily and often. Sin is at the door always to defile a man. Once defiled and there is sin and iniquity, a curse has glue to stick to a man. When there is a curse at least one demon is sent to enforce the curse and oppress, abuse, assault or steal from a man.

He strung His bow and set me as the target for His arrow. (Lam 3:12, HCSB, NASB, NET, LEB)

But the Lord is a man of war; the Lord is His name. He will not leave us twisting in the wind, He will arise and come to fight our battles with us, more than just *for* us, but He will not leave us alone for the enemy to take full advantage of us.

His hands are covered with lightning that he commands to strike his designated target. (Job 36:32 HCSB, ISV, NASB, NET, AM, LEB, WEB, ISV, NET)

Your bow was exposed, and your arrows targeted by command, (Hab 3:9 ISV)

Indeed, I'm going to stir up and bring against Babylon a great company of nations from the land of the north. They'll deploy for battle against her, and from there she will be captured. Their arrows will be like a skilled warrior; they won't miss their targets. (Jeremiah 50:9 ISV)

The Lord has weapons of war. He has a mighty army and in that army there are skilled archers and mighty ones who can wield their swords.

2. Archers of the Lord, shoot at those who are shooting at me, in the Name of Jesus.

3. Aim and shoot with skill and precision as Jehu against Jehoram and against Jezebel, for these arrows coming at me are from the evil human agents in the darkness; they are witchcraft, in the Name of Jesus.

Jehu aimed his bow and shot an arrow right between Jehoram's shoulders. The arrow went through his heart and he fell to his knees in his chariot. (2 Kings 9:24 NET)

Saints of God, for warfare, you have to be courageous, brave, even very courageous. You have to, in the whole armor of God stand, and stand, therefore.

Instead, you will put them to flight when you aim your bow at their faces. (Psalm 21:12 HCSB, ISV, NASB, AM, LEB, WEB)

Warfare can include breaking into the enemy's armory and stealing or destroying the weapons that they plan to use against you. We are speaking spirits, so our warfare includes speaking, praying, saying, decreeing and declaring if we are in our right position and authority in Christ. Therefore, we can pray and ask the Lord to help us.

4. Lord, make the enemy's arrows against me useless, in the Name of Jesus.

They will vanish like water that flows by; they will aim their useless arrows.
(Psalm 58:7HCSB)

Sharpen the arrows! Fill the quivers! The Lord has put it into the mind of the kings of the Medes because His plan is aimed at Babylon to destroy her, for it is the Lord's vengeance, vengeance for His temple.(Jeremiah 51:11 HCSB)

Ultimately, vengeance belongs to the Lord.

5. Lord, arise and take vengeance on my spiritual enemies who are also

Your enemies, that are influencing evil men in the natural to target me, in the Name of Jesus.

Let them melt away as waters that flow off; when he aimeth his arrows, let them be as blunted (Psalm 58:7 DARBY, ASV)

6. Make haste to defend me, Lord. Have Your Angels aim their bows, aim their arrows, aim their swords, aim their mighty weapons at those who are aiming at me, in the Name of Jesus.

Let them flow away like water that runs off; When he aims his arrows, let them be as headless shafts.(Psalm 58:7)

All of this seems well and good, but first we have to know that we are under attack or under siege. That is known in prayer where your spiritual sensitivity is attuned. That is known by the Holy Spirit. That is known by proper Christian interpretation of dreams which is the spirit realm, and you are in it every night. The Holy Spirit is talking to you, guiding you, teaching you, leading you, showing you.

Now that you know you are under attack, you need to know what to do. First, who are you under attack from? If it is not God, then there is hope for you. If it is any other evil entity or evil human agent, you are going to have to engage in spiritual warfare. When we look again at Job, if he thought an enemy combatant was attacking him, his response would have been far different than it was when he thought it was God. The fact that he didn't curse God or turn his back on God showed the immense love and respect Job had for God. Only the unwise would attempt warfare against God, so that is why Job seems so passive for 42 chapters.

And, that is why Lucifer and his crew got kicked out of Heaven.

The same would be true for any of us if we think it is God pruning us, teaching us, putting us through the purifying refiner's fire, chastening us, we respond differently than if we clearly know this is an enemy who came to steal, kill, and destroy.

We must know something about how these enemies are doing what they are doing to you? What weapon or weapons they are using. We should know why, and often through whom, although we don't take this battle to flesh.

And we must know on what authority do they have to do this? Have you forgotten or forsaken God?

And you have forgotten Yahweh, your maker, who stretched out [the] heavens, and founded [the] earth. And

you tremble continually, all day,
because of the wrath of the oppressor
when he {takes aim} to destroy. But
where [is] the wrath of the oppressor?
(Isaiah 51:13 LEB)

If the enemies are trespassing
and illegally attacking you, then you
must run to God in the Courts of Heaven
and report them. If the enemies of God
are legally attacking you, then run to
God immediately. REPENT. Repent
right away and then take to the
battlefield.

Who sharpen their tongues like
swords and aim bitter words like
arrows, (Psalm 64:3HCSB, ISV, NET, AM,
WEB)

This book is spiritual warfare
against enemy combatants, so we put on
the whole armor, cover ourselves in the
Blood of Jesus, and here we go.

What Is An Arrow?

Hear my voice, O God, in my prayer: preserve my life from fear of the enemy. Hide me from the secret counsel of the wicked; from the insurrection of the workers of iniquity: Who whet their tongue like a sword, *and* bend *their bows to shoot* their arrows, *even* bitter words: **That they may shoot in secret at the perfect: suddenly do they shoot at him, and fear not.** They encourage themselves *in* an evil matter: they commune of laying snares privily; they say, Who shall see them? They search out iniquities; they accomplish a diligent search: both the inward *thought* of every one *of them,* and the heart, *is* deep. But God shall shoot at them *with* an arrow; suddenly shall they be wounded.(Psalm 64:4-7)

When we hear the word, *arrow,* we may think it is the thing that is shot from a stringed bow or nowadays from a crossbow. By *arrow*, we are talking about a spiritual weapon. And, as devastating as physical weapons can be, spiritual weapons are mightier. Spiritual weapons can affect and penetrate multiple realms, and simultaneously.

When you affect the realm of the spirit, you affect everything. The spirit is the main thing, and it affects the lesser things. I can say that because you can change something in the physical realm, but if you don't also change it in the spiritual realm, it will revert back to whatever is in the spiritual realm. Every time.

You can give a man with a headache an analgesic such as aspirin or ibuprofen, but if that is a spiritual headache, the aspirin won't fix it--, it may fix it temporarily by blocking the symptoms, but that headache will persist. It will be back. You can give a man with no money, cold hard cash, but if the spiritual reason as to why he has no money is not fixed, he will still not have money.

You can spellcheck your friend's essay for school, but that won't teach them how to spell. You fixed the problem on that paper, but if they spiritually don't have the Wisdom or Knowledge of how to spell certain words—well, there you go.

Let it be done on Earth as it is in Heaven.

> Your kingdom come, your will be done, on earth as it is in heaven.
> (Matthew 6:10, ESV)

There is a leader, and there is a follower. The spirit realm leads, the physical world follows. Not only does it follow by being lower in rank and authority, and power--, it is also slower.

Yes & Amen

The promises of God are Yes and Amen.

For all the promises of God in him are yea, and in him Amen, unto the glory of God by us. (2 Corinthians 1:20)

That is how God answers your prayers--, Yes, and Amen. But where is the stuff that God already said, Yes, and Amen to?

It's tied up somewhere between the spirit realm and the physical realm. (one of the main reasons why is because God and the angels are in agreement with blessing mankind in the Third

Heaven, so the release of blessings is smooth fast and glorious.)

By the time the blessing that God is sending you gets to Second Heaven, that's where the bottleneck is. That's why things get slow, it's all the hindrances, obstacles, and barriers erected in the spirit realm against a person being blessed.

This is why we have and need altars. Altars are the interface between the two realms. The spirit realm – Third Heaven if you are serving God, as you should be. Godly altars connect us to God, and to the things of God.

Evil altars connect man to evil and to the kingdom of darkness.

So, the promises of God are YES and AMEN. He has already done everything for us. He has already given us everything. So, what's the delay? What's the holdup? We know why there is a traffic jam between spirit and physical, so the question is how do we fix it?

An altar. A Godly altar is how it is fixed. Amen. So, you've figured that out already? You've sorted that out ? AMEN.

Active Shooter

But there can be a new problem added to the mix. Now, while you are going to get the stuff you need for life and for godliness, there are evil entities and evil agents (who work for them) who now want to make you their target.

Surely a lion knows when the buffalo are going to the stream to drink. So, it comes to drink there also, and also hiding, the lion may crouch to attack, to feed.

The enemies of our souls know that we must go to God to get the things He has promised us and our daily bread, blessings, … everything. So, when do you think he may try to intercept? When we are distracted by daily life and daily living. When we are distracted by our flesh, especially.

> Hear my voice, O God, in my prayer: preserve my life from fear of the enemy. Hide me from the secret counsel of the wicked; from the insurrection of the workers of iniquity: Who whet their tongue like a sword, *and* bend *their bows to shoot* their arrows, *even* bitter words: **That they may shoot in secret at the perfect: suddenly do they shoot at him, and fear not.** They encourage themselves *in* an evil matter: they commune of laying snares privily;

Why do the evil shoot at the upright of God?

- They are evil. They are not of God and do not love or even like the things or people of God.
- They are ignorant, rebellious looking for mischief. Some will

get into evil for free—for no pay.

- They have been incentivized to do so. They have been told that there is something in it for them.
- They are thieves, they may shoot at the guy who is going to pick up his new TV or whatever, so they can snatch that TV from the guy who it belongs to.
- Accidentally – can't shoot straight, or didn't even know they were shooting, or that they were shooting at actual people. They could be Intoxicated, inebriated, initiated, indoctrinated, dedicated, medicated, not thinking. Not thinking straight, at all.

What are these arrows again?

Evil arrows represent demonic attacks or afflictions designed to harm, distract, or destroy lives and destinies. They are sent as curses, spells, hexes, vexes, jinxes--, that sort of thing. There are two categories of arrows: Arrows of affliction and arrows of death. You don't want either.

On Warfare Prayer Channel there is a prayer entitled, **Every Evil Arrow**. Dr. Olukoya listed 70 different evil arrows, but I believe the Holy Spirit gave me more than that to pray against—they are in that prayer.

The source of the evil arrow is the kingdom of darkness who influences, incites, pays, or tricks evil human agents to agree with their plans.

Nothing from the spiritual can happen on Earth unless at least one person agrees with the spirit – good or bad. God gave Earth to man, so nothing can happen here unless at least one of us agrees with the spirit realm.

Not agreeing with Heaven so that blessings, especially your own blessings, can come to you is like standing at a toll plaza and not letting anyone come through. It would be always wise to **agree** with God, agree with Heaven. So, at the toll plaza or gate is every car or truck you just love, but you don't feel like opening up the gate to let them through. Remember the promises of God are Yes and Amen. The promises of God are exceeding, great and precious promises. Don't you want them? Your mouth is the Gate in this case—open it, pray, say, decree, and declare and agree with Heaven with what comes out of your mouth.

When evil agents agree with the kingdom of darkness, we get hell's agenda on Earth. There are supposed to be more Christians than non-Christians on Earth, so how is hell allowed to come through the toll plaza?

Or, did we not *feel like* going to work today?

When we don't pray for whatever reason, there is either no agreement or not enough agreement to let the blessings come through.

Do you think an evil human agent will say, Oh, I don't feel like being diabolical today, maybe tomorrow? NO, they are hell bent on bringing hell to their victims. They like it when their targets are hit.

Some don't sleep, they can't sleep until they do harm to someone. Else: they, themselves will be harmed.

Why might a person pick another for a target?

- Jealousy – cain did it to abel
- Saul did it to David
- Greedy Jezebel did it to Naboth
- Covetous

- Power struck – Absalom to David
- Herod wanted to attack Jesus but couldn't locate Jesus.
- Filled with hatred – they could hate Christians for example. Hate you, your *type,* or any random thing about you.
- <u>Must</u> do it; they are contracted with the devil to do it.
- OR: Just for fun, to see what will hit. To see if curses and spells really work.

Or, they have quotas so they may shoot at random. They may have to reach a quota to jump into a coven.

This is why we don't keep bad company, it's so we won't receive collateral damage.

For no logical reason at all—your sunglasses are really cute. That could set someone off. Your hair is looking really good today – that might inflame a jealous soul.

Man of God, you've got a pretty wife and a BMW. That could put you on someone's list in such as simple way as they don't want you to get anything else nice. They want your wife to leave. They want your car to break down. Even those tiny, stupid, childish wishes are agreements with the kingdom of darkness. Those tiny, petty, evil wishes give legal right to shootists coming into a man's life.

And this is why we must stay prayed up all the time. We don't know who is shooting the side eye, or an evil eye in our direction.

According to our Scripture passage, this is all done in secret, so you don't know if they did it, when they did it, why they did it, how they did it – you just see the results when things start going sideways, or you get losses, or delays, or bad things happening when good things should be happening for you and in your life, in your home, in your marriage, children, and family.

That they may shoot in secret at the perfect: suddenly do they shoot at him, and fear not.

They aren't even afraid of doing this because they are hidden and know they are hidden. That is why it is called occult, or occultic. On top of that they are in a team, a group such as a coven. People always think they are safe when in numbers. Note the verse says that: They encourage themselves *in* an evil matter: they commune of laying snares privily; they say, Who shall see them?

They are in an echo chamber of sorts. One wants to do a bad thing, then the next, and the next, all agree. Soon they all agree and then they secretly lay traps. They are working together; there is much power in **agreement**.

Christians: are we? How many people can you get to join a prayer meeting?

So, don't be paranoid but an evil human agent could send out an arrow for no reason at all.

Years ago, I went to a wedding as a plus one. Never saw the bride nor the groom before. As the wedding started the bride--, she was beautiful, but as she took her first step to walk down the aisle, with her dad, she shot me an evil eye as if I had something that belonged to her. I did not, and I don't to this day know what that was about.

You don't have to do anything to people for them to decide to do something to you. You could just look like or remind them of something that hurt or traumatized them, and they've never healed from it. This could be why Jesus said to Agree with your adversary quickly. In addition, pray the Lord to restore your soul, so you don't harbor old stuff in there and take it out on innocent people.

Don't be paranoid, be wise. Be circumspect. Continue to walk upright before the Lord, as much as it is in you, by help of the Holy Spirit. Be full of the Fruit of the Spirit. **Repent always**. Pray without ceasing and stay under the Shadow of the Almighty.

Repent! Why do I have to repent? Our foundational Scripture reads that
They search out iniquities; they accomplish a diligent search: both the inward *thought* of every one *of them*, and the heart, *is* deep. (Psalm 64:6)

They are looking for the iniquity in another person which gives them permission to shoot. These searches are carried out by *monitoring* and *familiar spirits*.

Jesus said, **The prince of this world cometh and he has nothing in Me**.

I will not say much more to you, for the prince of this world is coming. He has no hold over me, (NIV)

I don't have much more time to talk to
you, because the ruler of this world
approaches. He has no power over me,
(NLT)

I will no longer talk much with you,
for the ruler of this world is coming.
He has no claim on me, (ESV)

Nobody shot an evil arrow at
Jesus. They couldn't. But what they did
was to try to get Jesus' own words to
condemn Him. So, as we look at what
other target hunters might be doing, do
not let your own words sabotage you.

Nobody stoned Jesus: they
couldn't. They picked up rocks to stone
Him, but they didn't because Jesus got
away. Jesus was never sick, didn't have
a cold, nothing--- because no arrows
could be fired at Him. Not arrows of
affliction nor a death arrow. No man
took His life; He laid it down.

Evil is out there. Let's leave it out
there.

But God–, there are evil archers and shootists out there. But God has Archers and Arrows too.

But God shall shoot at them *with* an arrow; suddenly shall they be wounded. (Psalm 64:7)

Saints of God, you must **agree** with that Scripture verse, you've got to agree with God. You have that authority in the Earth to let God's will be done in your life and in your circumstances or not. If you don't agree and **say** it, then there is no agreement.

How are we saved? We believe with our hearts and confess with our mouths. We must **say** what we believe to get the results we should receive.

So, I can recommend at least two prayers so you can agree with God regarding giving Him permission to defend you against evil arrows. Prayers for this message are: *Every Evil Arrow* & *I'm Not Your Target, Warfare*

Prayers Against Haters and the Powers they Employ. Both are on Warfare Prayer Channel on You Tube. https://www.youtube.com/@warfareprayerchannel3853

Following is the near-exact transcription of the prayer: **I AM NOT YOUR TARGET:** *Prayers Against Haters and the Powers they Employ.*

*Regarding these prayers, can you see how stopping shooters in the spirit will translate in every way to stop shooters in the natural realm? That which is spiritual regulates and delegates what happens in the natural. So be safe in both realms by praying these prayers.

I AM NOT YOUR TARGET

7. Son of David, have Mercy on me, a sinner. If I am none of Yours give me a repentant heart and godly sorrow for my sins and make me one of Yours, in the Name of Jesus.
8. Holy Spirit FIRE, fall, in the Name of Jesus. Holy Spirit Fire fall on these prayers, in the Name of Jesus.
9. In Him we move and breathe and have our being. Amen.

For in him we live, and move, and have our being; as certain also of your own poets have said, For we are also his offspring. (Acts 17:29)

And God formed man out of the clay of the Earth, breathed in him and he became a living soul. And God breathed in you, and you became a living soul.

10. Anyone who despises your being, let the Lord rebuke them, in the Name of Jesus.

Preach the word; be instant in season, out of season; reprove, rebuke, exhort with all longsuffering and doctrine. (2 Timothy 4:2)

The Lord *rebuke* thee, O Satan
(Zechariah 3:2, Isaiah 17:13)

11. Workers of iniquity, the LORD rebuke thee. The LORD reprove thee, in the Name of Jesus.
12. Evil human agents and persecutors, the LORD rebuke thee, chasten thee, check thee, punish thee, in the Name of Jesus.
13. Those that target me, Lord silence them, silence their words and enchantments against me, in the Name of Jesus. Break their power to

work against me, in the Name of Jesus.

14. Lord, rebuke in Thy hot displeasure, anyone, any entity or power that is targeting me, in the Name of Jesus.

15. I am not your target.

16. Lord, destroy the power, the altars, the thrones of anyone targeting me, by the power of Your Thunder and Lightnings, in the Name of Jesus.

17. I decree and declare in the heavenlies that I am not a candidate for evil, I'm not a candidate for loss, I am not a candidate for affliction, disappointment, sacrifice, or destruction of any kind, in the Name of Jesus. I am the Righteousness of God in Christ Jesus. I bear in my body the marks of the Lord Jesus Christ. I abide under the shadow of the Almighty, in the Name of Jesus.

18. Evil entities, I am not your candidate.

19. Evil agents, I am not your candidate.

20. I am not your target.

21. Anyone who has targeted me, for any reason, caused or causeless, I am not your target, in the Name of Jesus.

22. I'm not your target; even if you are mighty, I shall not be your prey, by the power in the Christ that I serve, the Lord God's Christ, in the Name of Jesus.

23. Anyone who has targeted me because I breathe, the Lord Jesus Christ rebuke you.

24. God has breathed life into me, and I live. I move. And I have being by the Grace of God, in the Name of Jesus.

25. Anyone who has targeted me because I exist, the Lord Jesus Christ check you, restrain you, constrain you from targeting me, I am God's property—the offspring of God.

Forasmuch then as we are the offspring of God, (Acts 17:29A)

Personal Attacks

26. Anyone who has targeted me because they don't like the way I look, the Lord Jesus Christ rebuke you.

27. Anyone who has targeted me because of the way I speak, the Lord Jesus Christ rebuke you. For the Lord has given me the tongue of the learned, in the Name of Jesus.

The Lord God hath given me the tongue of the learned, that I should know how to speak a word in season to him that is weary: he wakeneth morning by morning, he wakeneth mine ear to hear as the learned. (Isaiah 50:4)

28. I speak with the tongues of men and angels and I HAVE LOVE, in the Name of Jesus. (1 Corinthians 13:1)

29. Anyone who has targeted me because of the way I speak, the Lord Jesus Christ rebuke you. My tongue is the pen of the ready writer, in the Name of Jesus.

My heart is indicting a good matter: I speak of the things which I have made touching the king: my tongue *is* the pen of a ready writer. (Psalm 45:1)

30. Anyone who has targeted me, for any reason, caused or causeless, I am not your target, I am not your target, in the Name of Jesus.

31. Anyone who has targeted me because they don't like my nose, the LORD Jesus Christ rebuke you.

32. Anyone who has targeted me because they don't like my skin, the color, the texture, the tone, the Lord Jesus Christ rebuke you, in the Name of Jesus.

33. Anyone who has targeted me because they don't like my race, the

Lord Jesus Christ rebuke you, in the Name of Jesus.

34. Anyone who has targeted me because they don't like my culture, the LORD Jesus Christ rebuke you, in the Name of Jesus.

35. Anyone who has targeted me because they don't like my socio-economic position, the LORD Jesus Christ rebuke you, in the Name of Jesus.

36. Anyone who has targeted me because they don't like my ethnicity, the LORD Jesus Christ rebuke you, in the Name of Jesus.

37. Anyone who has targeted me because they don't like my hair, the color, the texture, the length, the style--, the LORD JESUS prohibit you from targeting me, in the Name of Jesus. My hair is my glory, in the Name of Jesus.

38. Anyone who has targeted me because they don't like my size, the Lord Jesus Christ rebuke you.

39. Anyone who has targeted me because they don't like my weight, the Lord Jesus Christ rebuke you.

40. Anyone who has targeted me because they don't like my lack of weight, the Lord Jesus Christ rebuke you.

41. Anyone who has targeted me because they don't like my style, my swag, the Lord Jesus Christ rebuke you.

42. Anyone who has targeted me because they don't like my mind, the Lord Jesus Christ rebuke you. I have the Mind of Christ, I can know all things, I can remember all things, in Christ by the Holy Spirit. Amen.

43. Anyone who has targeted me because they don't like my eyes, the Lord Jesus Christ rebuke you.

44. Anyone who has targeted me because they don't like my eyelashes, the Lord Jesus Christ rebuke you.

45. Anyone who has targeted me because they don't like my eyebrows, the Lord Jesus Christ rebuke you.

46. Anyone who has targeted me because they don't like my intelligence, the Lord Jesus Christ rebuke you. The Lord would not have you ignorant, so I study to show myself approved, a workman who need not be ashamed, in the Name of Jesus.

47. Anyone who has targeted me because they don't like my sense of humor, the Lord Jesus Christ rebuke you.

Relationships

48. Anyone who has targeted me because they don't like my boyfriend, the Lord Jesus Christ rebuke you. Divine connections are made by God with purpose and destiny in mind.

49. Anyone who has targeted me because they don't like my girlfriend, the Lord Jesus Christ rebuke you. Divine connections are made by God with purpose and destiny in mind.

50. Anyone who has targeted me because they are coveting my boyfriend or girlfriend, the LORD Jesus Christ, rebuke you, in the Name of Jesus. Divine connections are made by God with purpose and destiny in mind. Amen.

51. Anyone who has targeted me because they are coveting my spouse, the LORD Jesus Christs rebuke you, in the Name of Jesus. Strange man, strange woman, you are rebuked, in the Name of Jesus.

52. Anyone who has targeted me because they don't like my family, the LORD Jesus Christ rebuke you, in the Name of Jesus.

53. Anyone targeting me because they don't like that I have a family, the LORD Jesus Christ rebuke you, in the Name of Jesus.

54. Anyone who has targeted me because they don't like my mother, the Lord Jesus Christ rebuke you.

55. Anyone who has targeted me because they don't like my father, the Lord Jesus Christ rebuke you.

56. Anyone who has targeted me because they don't like my aunt, the Lord Jesus Christ rebuke you.

57. Anyone who has targeted me because they don't like my uncle, the Lord Jesus Christ rebuke you.

58. Anyone who has targeted me because they don't like my grandmother, the Lord Jesus Christ rebuke you.

59. Anyone who has targeted me because they don't like my grandfather, the Lord Jesus Christ rebuke you.

60. Anyone targeting me because they don't like any of my relatives, the LORD Jesus Christ rebuke you, in the Name of Jesus.

61. Anyone targeting me because they don't like one or some, or any of my relatives, the Lord Jesus Christ rebuke you. in the Name of Jesus.

62. The Lord has put the solitary in families by divine appointment, purpose and destiny, in the Name of Jesus.

My House

63. Anyone who has targeted me because they don't like my house--, it's too nice or not good enough--, the Lord Jesus Christ rebuke you. In my Father's house there are many mansions; in the Earth realm, there are many houses and the Lord provides.
64. Anyone who has targeted me because they don't like my yard, the Lord Jesus Christ rebuke you.
65. Anyone targeting me just because you're petty, the LORD Jesus Christ chasten and reprove you, in the Name of Jesus.

Spiritual Matters

66. Anyone who has targeted me because they don't like my relationship with God, the Lord Jesus Christ rebuke you.

67. Anyone who has targeted me because they don't like My prayer life, the Lord Jesus Christ rebuke you. The prayers of the righteous availeth much.

68. Anyone who has targeted me because they don't like my conversations, the Lord Jesus Christ rebuke you.

69. Anyone who has targeted me because they don't like that I have a husband, the Lord Jesus Christ rebuke you. Spirit of *anti-marriage,*

be bound from operating in my life and marriage, in the Name of Jesus.

70. Anyone who has targeted me because they don't like my wife, the Lord Jesus Christ rebuke you. Spirit of *anti-marriage*, be bound from operating in my life and marriage, in the Name of Jesus.

71. Anyone who has targeted me because they don't like My kids, the Lord Jesus Christ rebuke you. Lord put a shield of protection around my children and protect them day and night, in the Name of Jesus. Children are a heritage from the LORD; I will never despise my heritage. The Blood of Jesus is between me and you--, you *targeter,* and between you and my kids, in the Name of Jesus.

72. Anyone who has targeted me because they don't like my grandkids, the Lord Jesus Christ rebuke you.

Pettiness

73. Anyone who has targeted me because they don't like my cooking, the Lord Jesus Christ rebuke you.
74. Anyone who has targeted me because they don't like my garden, or my gardening or that I have a garden, the Lord Jesus Christ rebuke you.
75. Anyone targeting me for any petty reason, the Lord Jesus Christ rebuke you.
76. Anyone who has targeted me because they don't like my car, or that I have a car, or that I have the car that I have, the Lord Jesus Christ rebuke you.

77. Anyone who has targeted me because they don't like my truck, the Lord Jesus Christ rebuke you.

78. Anyone who has targeted me because they don't like my dog, the Lord Jesus Christ rebuke you.

79. Anyone who has targeted me because they don't like my cat, the Lord Jesus Christ rebuke you.

80. Anyone who has targeted me because they don't like My goldfish or any pet I have, the Lord Jesus Christ rebuke you, in the Name of Jesus.

Education

81. Anyone who has targeted me because they don't like my education, the Lord Jesus Christ rebuke you.

82. Anyone who has targeted me because they don't like that I don't have education or the same education that they have, the Lord Jesus Christ rebuke you. The Lord sits High and He looks down low, in the Name of Jesus.

83. Anyone who has targeted me because they don't like my intelligence, the Lord Jesus Christ rebuke you.

84. Anyone who has targeted me because they don't like my wit, the Lord Jesus Christ rebuke you.
85. Anyone who has targeted me because they don't like my playfulness or my seriousness, the Lord Jesus constrain you, in the Name of Jesus.

Destiny

86. Anyone who has targeted me because they don't like my vision, the Lord Jesus Christ rebuke you.

Without a vision, the people perish,
(Proverbs 18:29A)

87. Anyone who has targeted me because they don't like my spiritual gifts, the Lord Jesus Christ rebuke you.

88. Anyone who has targeted me because they don't like my destiny, the Lord Jesus Christ rebuke you. They hated Joseph's dreams, but I must fulfill destiny.

89. Anyone who has targeted me because they don't like my plans, the Lord Jesus Christ rebuke you.

90. Anyone who has targeted me because they don't like my favor, the Lord Jesus Christ rebuke you.

Surely, Lord, you bless the righteous; you surround them with your favor as with a shield. (Psalms 5:12)

91. Anyone who has targeted me because they don't like my wallet, and whatever you think I have in it, the Lord Jesus Christ rebuke you.

92. Anyone who has targeted me because they don't like what they think I have in my wallet, the Lord Jesus Christ rebuke you, in the Name of Jesus.

93. Anyone who has targeted me because they don't like my bank account, jealous of it, or thinking it is not enough to warrant respect, the Lord Jesus Christ rebuke you.

94. Anyone who has targeted me because they don't like my retirement fund, or that I am retired, or able to retire, the Lord Jesus Christ rebuke you.

95. Anyone who has targeted me because they don't like my credit cards, or that I have them, the Lord Jesus Christ rebuke you.

96. Anyone who has targeted me because they don't like my credit rating, or what they think is my credit rating, the Lord Jesus Christ silence you, in the Name of Jesus.

97. Anyone who has targeted me because they don't like My vacations, the Lord Jesus Christ rebuke you.

98. Anyone who has targeted me because they don't like my travel, the Lord Jesus Christ rebuke you. It is the Lord that empowers us to get wealth and to enjoy it, in the Name of Jesus.

99. The Earth is the Lord's and the fulness therof, and it is full of His glory and His majesty. Hc is my Father, in the Name of Jesus.

100. Anyone who has targeted me because they don't like my birthday, or that I'm celebrated at any time, for any reason, the Lord Jesus Christ rebuke you.

101. Anyone who has targeted me because they don't like my parties, get togethers or gatherings, or meetings, the Lord Jesus Christ rebuke you.

102. Anyone who has targeted me because they don't like my ministry, the Lord Jesus Christ silence you and rebuke you, in the Name of Jesus.

103. Lord, rebuke the jealous, rebuke the petty, rebuke the competitive and remove them from my life, in the Name of Jesus, so that I may move and breathe, and have *being*, to the

praise of Your glory, Hallelujah. (X2 or more)

104. Anyone targeting me with foolish or sinful distractions, take your distractions and go, leave me now. Go, leave me now, in the Name of Jesus.

105. Anyone or any entity tempting me with sin, the LORD break your power over me, in the Name of Jesus.

106. Anyone who has targeted me because they don't like my online presence, the Lord Jesus Christ rebuke you, in the Name of Jesus.

107. Anyone who has targeted me because I put too much information online, Lord, forgive me and hide me from targeting, evil *monitoring spirits* and eyes, in the Name of Jesus.

108. Any *monitoring spirit* who has targeted me because I won't post my business online and is angry, because they can't find out what it is--, the

Lord break your assignment and power over my life, in the Name of Jesus.

109. Lord, break the power and the assignment these evil *spirits* have over my life, in the Name of Jesus.

The Thief

110. Anyone who has targeted me because they think I have something that belongs to them, or that I've taken something that belongs to them, the Lord Jesus Christ rebuke you, in the Name of Jesus. The thief comes not but to steal, kill, and destroy: I AM NOT A THIEF, I am not the thief.

111. Anyone who has targeted me because they don't like my décor or holiday decorations, the Lord Jesus Christ rebuke you.

112. Anyone who has targeted me because they don't like my clothes, the Lord Jesus Christ rebuke you.

113. Anyone who has targeted me because they don't like my tops, my bottoms, my suits, my dresses, my shirts, my accessories--, the Lord Jesus Christ rebuke you.

114. Lord, let my adornment be not just on the outside, but inward as well, (1 Peter 3:3)

115. Anyone who has targeted me because they don't like my jewelry, watches or anything that I wear or use, the Lord Jesus Christ rebuke you.

116. Anyone who has targeted me because they believe that my cellphone is too good for me, or that I have a cellphone that they think is better than their cellphone—any petty person, the Lord Jesus Christ rebuke you, in the Name of Jesus

117. Anyone who has targeted me because they don't like my perfume, cologne or other fragrance, the Lord Jesus rebuke you, in the Name of Jesus.

118. Anyone who has targeted me because they don't like my furniture, the Lord Jesus Christ rebuke you.

119. Anyone who has targeted me because they think my furniture is too nice, the Lord Jesus Christ rebuke you.

120. Anyone who has targeted me because they don't like my closet, or what is in it, the Lord Jesus Christ rebuke you.

121. Anyone who has targeted me because they don't like my bathroom, whether you love it, hate it, or wish you had one like it, the Lord Jesus Christ rebuke you.

122. Anyone who has targeted me because they don't like my kitchen, whether you think it is beneath you,

or too good for me, the Lord Jesus
Christ rebuke you.

123. Anyone who has targeted me
because they don't like my
appliances, the label, the name
brand, the quality or the lack thereof,
the Lord Jesus Christ rebuke you. I
will never despise small beginnings,
in the Name of Jesus.

124. Anyone who has targeted me
because they don't like my garage, or
what's in it, the Lord Jesus Christ
rebuke you.

125. Anyone who has targeted me
because they don't like that I have
recreational vehicles, the Lord Jesus
Christ rebuke you.

126. Anyone who has targeted me
because they don't like that I have
tools and instruments, the Lord Jesus
Christ rebuke you.

127. Anyone who has targeted me
because they don't like my driveway,
the Lord Jesus Christ rebuke you.

128.   Anyone who doesn't even know me, but has targeted me, the Lord Jesus Christ rebuke you, in the Name of Jesus.

Spiritual Gifts

129.   Anyone who has targeted me because they don't like my joy, the Lord Jesus Christ rebuke you.

For the kingdom of God is not meat and drink; but righteousness, and peace, and joy in the Holy Ghost.
(Romans 14:17)

130.   Anyone who has targeted me because they don't like My peace, the God of Peace will soon crush Satan under my feet, in the Name of Jesus.

And the God of peace shall bruise Satan under your feet shortly. The grace of our Lord Jesus Christ *be* with you. Amen (Romans 16:20)

131. Anyone who has targeted me because they don't like my happiness, the Lord Jesus Christ rebuke you.

132. Anyone who has targeted me because they don't like my contentment, the Lord Jesus Christ rebuke you.

133. Anyone who has targeted me because I am not suffering, lose all power against me, in the Name of Jesus. (X2)

134. Anyone who has targeted me because I am whole, lose all your power against me, in the Name of Jesus.

135. Anyone who has targeted me because I am delivered and set free in Christ, lose all your power against me, in the Name of Jesus.

136. Anyone who has targeted me because I am not afflicted, instead of what you want to happen to me, may

may <u>you</u> receive what you desire to happen to me, in the Name of Jesus.

137. Anyone who has targeted me because they don't like my giving, the Lord Jesus Christ rebuke you. The Lord loves a cheerful giver, and I am loved by the Lord Jesus Christ. Amen.

138. Anyone who has targeted me because they don't like my receiving what the Lord has for me, the Lord Jesus Christ rebuke you. Those who sow in tears will come reaping in joy, in the Name of Jesus.

139. Anyone who has targeted me because they don't like my planting, the Lord Jesus Christ rebuke you. The sower sows the Word. I cast my bread up on the waters and after many days… Hallelujah.

Cast thy bread upon the waters: for thou shalt find it after many days.

Give a portion to seven, and also to
eight; for thou knowest not what evil
shall be upon the earth.
(Ecclesiastes 11:1-2)

140. Anyone who has targeted me
because they don't like my
harvesting, the Lord Jesus Christ
rebuke you.

141. Anyone who has targeted me
because they don't like my purpose,
the Lord Jesus Christ rebuke you. It
is God who has chosen me.

Ye have not chosen me, but I have
chosen you, and ordained you, that ye
should go and bring forth fruit, and
that your fruit should remain: that
whatsoever ye shall ask of the Father
in my name, he may give it you.
(John 15:16)

142. Anyone who has targeted me
because you don't like my *fruit*, the
Lord Jesus chastise you as it
concerns me, in the Name of Jesus.

143. Anyone who has targeted me
because they don't like my spiritual

gifts, the Lord Jesus Christ rebuke you. Or, you don't like that I have spiritual gifts, or the spiritual gifts that I have; the Lord Jesus Christ rebuke you.

The gifts and callings of God are without repentance (Romans 11:29)

Now there are diversities of gifts, but the same Spirit.

And there are differences of administrations, but the same Lord. (1 Corinthians 12:4-5)

144. Anyone who has targeted me because they don't like my confidence, and my boldness, the Lord Jesus Christ rebuke you.

In whom (Christ) we have boldness and access with confidence by the faith of him. (Ephesians 3:12).

I am in Christ.

145. Anyone who has targeted me because they don't like that I don't

have fear, the Lord Jesus Christ rebuke you.

146. Anyone who has targeted me because I lack fear, the Lord Jesus Christ rebuke you. The Lord has not given me a *spirit of fear,* but one of love, power, and of a sound mind. I shall not fear what man can do to me.

147. Anyone who has targeted me because they don't like my lack of worry, the Lord Jesus Christ rebuke you. The Word says to be careful for nothing, be anxious for nothing. I am not forsaken, I am in Christ. Amen.

148. Anyone who has targeted me because they don't like my smile, the Lord Jesus Christ rebuke you.

Thou shalt no more be termed Forsaken; neither shall thy land any more be termed Desolate: but thou shalt be called **Hephzibah,** and thy land Beulah: (Isaiah 62:4-5)

149. I'm not your target. I am not your target. The evil lie in wait to privily

shoot at the upright; their evil will not go unpunished; the Lord Jesus Christ rebuke you.

The Lord's Masterpiece

150. Anyone who has targeted me because they don't like my skills, the Lord Jesus Christ rebuke you.

151. Anyone who has targeted me because they don't like that I have witty inventions; those inventions are from the Lord. Father, protect your investment in me, in the Name of Jesus and remove any shootists from me and mine, in the Name of Jesus.

152. Anyone who has targeted me because they don't like my talents, the Lord Jesus Christ rebuke you. I am the Lord's masterpiece, (Ephesians 2:10). I am the Lord's masterpiece, Amen.

153. Anyone who has targeted me because they don't like my abilities, the Lord Jesus Christ rebuke you.

154. I am the Lord's masterpiece.

155. Anyone who has targeted me because they don't like my natural abilities, the Lord Jesus Christ rebuke you.

156. Anyone who has targeted me because they don't like my God-given abilities, the Lord Jesus Christ rebuke you. I am the LORD's masterpiece, created in Christ Jesus for good works, in the Name of Jesus. Amen. (Ephesians 2:10)

My Prayers

157. Anyone who has targeted me because they don't like my prayers, the Lord Jesus Christ rebuke you.

Likewise the Spirit also helpeth our infirmities: for we know not what we should pray for as we ought: but the Spirit itself maketh intercession for us with groanings which cannot be uttered.

And he that searcheth the hearts knoweth what is the mind of the Spirit, because he maketh intercession for the saints according to the will of God.
(Romans 8:26-28)

158. Anyone who has targeted me because they don't like my fasting, the Lord Jesus Christ check you from interfering with me, in the Name of Jesus.

159. Anyone who has targeted me because they don't like that I'm anointed of God; the Lord Jesus Christ rebuke you.

> And it shall come to pass in that day, that his burden shall be taken away from off thy shoulder, and his yoke from off thy neck, and the yoke shall be destroyed because of the anointing.
> (Isaiah 10:27)

159. Anyone who has targeted me because they don't like that God has glorified me with the glory that is due man, the Lord Jesus Christ rebuke you.

160. Anyone who has targeted me because of my soul; the Lord Jesus Christ rebuke you. I possess my soul in sanctification and honor, in the Name of Jesus.

161. Anyone attempting to steal my star or glory, let the glory of my star be your undoing, in the Name of Jesus.

162. Anyone who has targeted me because they don't like my Godly discipline, the Lord Jesus Christ rebuke you. My God is a rewarder of the diligent.

163. Anyone who has targeted me because they don't like my God, the Lord Jesus Christ rebuke you.

Hear the word of the LORD, ye that tremble at his word; Your brethren that hated you, that cast you out for my name's sake, said, Let the LORD be glorified: but he shall appear to your joy, and they shall be ashamed. (Isaiah 66:5)

164. Anyone who has targeted me because they don't like my Bible, the Lord Jesus Christ rebuke you.

In the beginning was the Word, and the Word was with God, and the Word was God. (John 1:1)

165. Anyone who has targeted me because they don't like my beliefs, the LORD Jesus Christ rebuke you.

My faith is built on nothing less than Jesus' Blood and Righteousness.

166. Anyone who has targeted me because they don't like my spirit – the spirit of the Lord God is upon me, I have the Spirit of God and the Mind of Christ.

167. Anyone who has targeted me because they don't like my praise, the Lord Jesus Christ rebuke you. God inhabits the praises of His people.

But thou art holy, O thou that inhabitest the praises of Israel.
(Psalm 22:3)

168. Anyone who has targeted me because they don't like my worship, the Lord Jesus Christ rebuke you. Man was made to worship the Lord. Amen.

169. Anyone who has targeted me because they don't like my voice, the Lord Jesus Christ restrain you.

170. Anyone who has targeted me because they don't like my words, the Lord Jesus Christ rebuke you. The angels of the Lord come for my words when I give voice to the Word of God. Amen.

171. Anyone who has targeted me because they don't like my writing or my handwriting, the Lord Jesus Christ rebuke you.

172. Anyone who has targeted me because they don't like my job or profession, the Lord Jesus Christ rebuke you.

173. Anyone who has targeted me because they don't like that I have a job or a profession, or a career, the Lord Jesus Christ rebuke you, in the Name of Jesus.

174. Anyone who has targeted me because they don't like my career, the Lord Jesus Christ rebuke you.

175. Anyone who has targeted me because they don't like my gender,

the Lord Jesus Christ rebuke you. I am fearfully and wonderfully made and that I know right well, in the Name of Jesus.

176. Anyone who has targeted me because they don't like my promotions, the Lord Jesus Christ rebuke you.

For promotion cometh neither from the east, nor from the west, nor from the south. But God is the judge: he putteth down one, and setteth up another. (Psalm 75:6-7)

177. Promotion comes from the Lord. Amen.

178. Anyone who has targeted me because they don't like My advancements, and my accomplishments, the Lord Jesus Christ rebuke you.

179. Anyone who has targeted me because they don't like my favor, the Lord Jesus Christ rebuke you. The favor of God is life and every

morning I get new mercies and daily loaded with benefits, in the Name of Jesus.

180.   Anyone who has targeted me because they don't like my blessings, the Lord Jesus Christ rebuke you. I am blessed going in and coming out. I am blessed in the city and blessed in the field. I am blessed when I sit down and blessed when I rise up. I am blessed and cannot be cursed; I am the head only, and not the tail. I am above only and not beneath. I am blessed and I cannot be cursed. Every curse, back to sender, in the Name of Jesus.

Thine own wickedness shall correct thee, and thy backslidings shall reprove thee: know therefore and see that it is an evil thing and bitter, that thou hast forsaken the LORD thy God that my fear *is* not in thee, saith the LORD GOD of Hosts. (Jeremiah 2:19)

Your wickedness will punish you;
your backsliding will rebuke you.
Consider then and realize
how evil and bitter it is for you
when you forsake the Lord your God
and have no awe of me,"
declares the Lord, the Lord Almighty.
(Jeremiah 2:19 NIV)

181. Anyone who has targeted me because they want to steal from me, **but can't**, the LORD Jesus Christ continue to restrain you by His rebuke, in the Name of Jesus.

He suffered no man to do them wrong: yea, he reproved kings for their sakes;

Saying, Touch not mine anointed, and do my prophets no harm. (1 Chronicles 16:21, Psalm 105:14-15)

182. Anyone who has targeted me because they've stolen from me in the past, but can no longer--, the LORD Jesus Christ check you by His hot rebuke, in the Name of Jesus.

183. Anyone who has targeted me because their devious plans and

devices did not work in the past, the Lord Jesus Christ rebuke you, in the Name of Jesus.

He frustrates the devices of the crafty,
So that their hands cannot carry out
their plans. (Job 5:12)

Dreams & Visions

184.   Anyone who has targeted me because they don't like my age, the Lord Jesus Christ rebuke you. Out of the mouth of babes God as ordained praise. God will pour out His Spirit on all flesh; the young men shall see visions and the old will dream dreams, in the Name of Jesus.

And it shall come to pass afterward, that I will pour out my spirit upon all flesh; and your sons and your daughters shall prophesy, your old men shall dream dreams, your young men shall see visions:

And also upon the servants and upon the handmaids in those days will I pour out my spirit.

And I will shew wonders in the heavens and in the earth, blood, and fire, and pillars of smoke. (Joel 2:28-32)

185. Anyone who has targeted me because they don't like my Wisdom, the Lord Jesus Christ rebuke you. If any lack Wisdom let him ask the Lord who will give it liberally, in the Name of Jesus.

If you need wisdom, ask our generous God, and he will give it to you. He will not rebuke you for asking.
(James 1:5, NLT)

186. Anyone who has targeted me because they don't like my youth, the Lord Jesus Christ constrain you, in the Name of Jesus.

187. Anyone who has targeted me because they don't like my hope for the future, the Lord Jesus Christ rebuke you.

188. Anyone who has targeted me because they don't like what they think or know I will be in the future,

the Lord Jesus Christ rebuke you, in the Name of Jesus.

189. I have been redeemed. I have been redeemed in Christ, in the Name of Jesus.

190. No devil, no demon, no spiritual entity and no evil human agent, can come against me, they have no rights to come against me because I have been redeemed. So, step back, fall back, get off me, I belong to Christ, in the Name of Jesus.

191. Anyone who has targeted me because they don't like my business, or that I have a business, or conduct business, or enjoy success and prosperity in business, the Lord Jesus Christ rebuke you.

192. Anyone who has targeted me because I am not suffering, lose all power against me, in the Name of Jesus. The Lord has not prepared me for the bread of sorrows or waters of affliction. Nor has he prepared for

me the bread of sorrows or the waters
of affliction, in the Name of Jesus.

Certificates & Diplomas

193. Anyone who has targeted me because they don't like my church that I go to or or that I go to church, the Lord Jesus Christ rebuke you.

194. Anyone who has targeted me because they don't like my position in church or life, the Lord Jesus Christ rebuke you.

195. Anyone who has targeted me because they don't like my titles, the Lord Jesus Christ rebuke you.

196. Anyone who has targeted me because they don't like my education or that I am educated, the Lord Jesus Christ rebuke you. Beloved, the LORD does not want us ignorant.

197. Anyone who has targeted me because they don't like my diplomas, degrees, and certificates, the Lord Jesus Christ rebuke you.

198. Anyone who has targeted me because they don't like my successes, the Lord Jesus Christ rebuke you.

199. Anyone who has targeted me because they don't like my accomplishments, the Lord Jesus Christ rebuke you. He that observes the wind will never sow, so just do what the Lord has instructed you to do. Amen.

200. Anyone who has targeted me because they don't like my favor, the Lord Jesus Christ rebuke you. I walk in Divine favor 24/7, in the Name of Jesus.

201. Anyone who has targeted me because they don't like my opportunities, the Lord Jesus Christ rebuke you.

For a great door and effectual is opened unto me, and *there are* many adversaries.(1 Corinthians 16:19)

202.   I pray the LORD will restrain you from targeting me, and may you turn to see your own open doors and stop worrying about mine, in the Name of Jesus.

Haters

203. Anyone who has targeted me because they want me to be hated, and I am not, the Lord Jesus Christ rebuke you, in the Name of Jesus.
204. Any sibling or relative who has targeted me with hate like Esau hated Jacob, or like Cain hated Abel, the Lord, Jesus rebuke you, in the Name of Jesus.

For *it was* not an
enemy *that* reproached me; then I
could have borne *it.* neither *was*
it he that **hated** me *that* did
magnify *himself* against me; then I
would have hid myself from him:
But *it was* you, a man my equal,

My companion and my
acquaintance. (Psalm 55:12-13)

205. Any brother in the faith who is
pretending and targeting me like
Judas targeted Jesus, I am not your
target, I am not your target. I am not
your target, the Lord Jesus rebuke
you, in the Name of Jesus.

206. Any sibling or brother who
cannot speak peaceably to me, the
Lord Jesus put a sword between you
and me, in the Name of Jesus.

207. Lord if I am hated needlessly and
without cause, instead give me favor
as you did for Leah who was hated,
in the Name of Jesus. (Genesis 29:31)

208. Lord, make me fruitful. Lord,
make me fruitful in every way, in the
Name of Jesus.

209. Anyone who has targeted me
because of my dream, I will not be
captured by you, in the Name of
Jesus.

210. Anyone who has targeted me because of my dream, I will not be put in your pit or well, in the Name of Jesus.

He that digs a pit shall fall into it himself, and I shall escape like a bird, in the Name of Jesus. (Gen 37:5)

211. Anyone who has targeted me because of my dream and I have told you my dream and so you hate me more, the Lord Jesus rebuke you and keep you away from me and my dreams, in the Name of Jesus, (Genesis 37:5, 8)

212. Anyone who has targeted me with evil arrows, as the archers who shot at Joseph because they hated him, the Lord Jesus Christ rebuke you, in the Name of Jesus (Genesis 49:23).

The archers have sorely grieved him, and shot *at him*, and **hated** him: (Genesis 49:23)

213. Any neighbor or person in close proximity to me that has targeted me for any reason, the blood of Jesus is between us, let the Lord Jesus Christ rebuke you, in the Name of Jesus, (Deuteronomy 4:42)

214. Anyone who has targeted me suddenly and was my friend before, the Lord Jesus Christ rebuke you and put a sword between me and you, in the Name of Jesus. (Deuteronomy 19:4, 6) (x2 or more)

215. Anyone who has targeted me because of my inheritance, the Lord Jesus Christ rebuke you, in the Name of Jesus. I am the seed of Abraham. I am in Isaac, I am in Jacob, I am an heir to the Promise, in Jesus Christ.

And if ye be Christ's, then are ye Abraham's seed, and heirs according to the promise. (Galatians 3:29)

216. Anyone who has targeted me because of hate, like Cain hated

Abel, like Saul hated David, the Lord
Jesus Christ rebuke you now, in the
Name of Jesus.

217.   Anyone who has targeted me
because they hate my soul or my
very being, the Lord Jesus Christ
rebuke you, in the Name of Jesus. (2
Samuel 5:8)

Money

218. Anyone who has targeted me because they owe me money and have turned on me, the Lord Jesus Christ rebuke you, in the Name of Jesus.

219. Anyone who hates me because they have offended or assaulted me and are now gaslighting, the Lord Jesus Christ rebuke you, in the Name of Jesus (2 Samuel 13:15)

220. Anyone who has targeted me because of hate like the way Absalom hated Amnon, the Lord Jesus Christ rebuke you.

And Absalom spake unto his brother
Amnon neither good nor bad: for
Absalom hated Amnon, because he had
forced his sister Tamar. (2 Samuel 13:22)

221. Lord, deliver me from my strong
enemy and from them that hate me; I
am not their target. I am not their
target, in the Name of Jesus.

222. Lord, deliver me from jealous
people, in the Name of Jesus.

223. Lord, deliver me from petty
people, in the Name of Jesus.

224. Lord, hide me in the cleft of the
Rock, in the Name of Jesus.

225. Lord, hide me under the shadow
of Your Wings, in the Name of Jesus.

226. Lord, Your Name is a strong
tower that I can run into and be safe,
in the Name of Jesus.

227. Lord, give Your Angels charge
over me to keep me in all of my
ways, so I don't even dash my foot
on a stone, in the Name of Jesus.

228. Anyone targeting me, know that there are more with me, than those that are with you, in the Name of Jesus.

229. Lord Jesus, I subdue my enemies by the power in the Name of Jesus Christ.

230. Lord, arise and trouble those who are troubling me, in the Name of Jesus.

231. Lord, arise and contend with those that contend with me, in the Name of Jesus.

He delivered me from
my strong enemy, *and* from them
that **hated** me: for they were too
strong for me. (2 Samuel 22:18)

232. **I AM NOT YOUR TARGET**, in the Name of Jesus.

233. Anyone who would target me, I am not your target.

234.   Any haters, I am not your target. Any enemies of God, I am not your target, in the Name of Jesus.

235.   LORD, LET ME HAVE RULE OVER THEM THAT **HATE** ME, in the NAME of Jesus. (Ester 9:1)... as you gave the Jews rule over them that hated them, in the Name of JESUS, let me have rule over them that hate me, in the Name of Jesus.

Thus, the Jews smote all their enemies with the stroke of the sword, and slaughter, and destruction, and did what they would unto those that **hated** them.
(Esther 9:5)

236.   I am not your target.

237.   Lord, arise and contend with those who contend with me, in the Name of Jesus.

He delivered me from my strong enemy, and from them which **hated** me: for they were too strong for me. (Psalm 18:17)

I have **hated** the congregation of evil doers; and will not sit with the wicked.
(Psalm 26:5)

238.   Anyone who has targeted me because they regard and believe lying vanities, know this: I trust in the Lord. I trust in the Lord. I trust in the Lord.

239.   Lord, rebuke them, in the Name of Jesus and render them powerless against me, in Jesus' Name.

I have **hated** them that regard lying vanities: but I trust in the LORD. (Psalm 31:6)

Lord, Send Correction

240. Anyone who has targeted me because they think that I have something that belongs to them, the Lord Jesus Christ rebuke you.

241. Anyone who has targeted me because they think that I have stolen from them, the Lord Jesus Christ send correction and rebuke you, now, in the Name of Jesus.

242. Anyone who has targeted me because they don't like something that they believe is true about me that may not even be true, the Lord Jesus Christ rebuke you, in the Name of

Jesus. Send correction in the Name
of Jesus.

243.   Anyone who has targeted me
because they hate me with or without
cause, Lord put them to shame, in the
Name of Jesus.

But thou hast saved us from our
enemies, and hast put them to
shame that hated us. (Psalm 44:7)

And he saved them from the hand of
him that hated *them*, and redeemed
them from the hand of the enemy.
(Psalm 106:10)

And he gave them into the hand of the
heathen; and
they that hated them ruled over them.

244.   Lord, do not let anyone who has
targeted me, have rule over me, in
the Name of Jesus. (Psalm 106:41)

245.   Any person of wicked devices
that has targeted me, the Lord put a
sword between me and you, in the
Name of Jesus. (Proverbs 14:17)

246.   Anyone who has targeted me, the Lord put a sword between me and you, in the Name of Jesus.

247.   Anyone who has targeted me because I am poor, the Lord Jesus rebuke you, in the Name of Jesus.

248.   Anyone who has targeted me because I am poor, Lord, rebuke them, in the Name of Jesus.

249.   Anyone who has targeted me because I am rich, the Lord Jesus Christ rebuke you, in the Name of Jesus.

250.   Anyone who has targeted me because they *think* I am rich, (Proverbs 14:20), the Lord Jesus Christ rebuke you.

251.   I command the defensive and offensive weapons of all my adversaries to fail and perish by the Blood of Jesus Christ.

252.   Lord, instead of being forsaken and hated because of being targeted by evil entities and agents--, instead,

Lord, make me an eternal excellency
and a joy of many generations, in the
Name of Jesus. (Isaiah 60:15)

Whereas thou hast
been forsaken and **hated,** so that no
man went through *thee,* I will make
thee an eternal excellency, a joy of
many generations. (Isaiah 60:15)

Exes

253. Anyone who has targeted me because they are my ex, the Lord Jesus rebuke you, in the Name of Jesus.

Behold, therefore I will gather all thy lovers, with whom thou hast taken pleasure, and all *them* that thou hast loved, with all *them* that thou hast **hated**; I will even gather them round about against thee, and will discover thy nakedness unto them, that they may see all thy nakedness. (Ezekiel 16:37)

254. Anyone who has targeted me because I rejected them, for whatever reason, Lord, do not let them bring me to shame or uncover

my nakedness, or disgrace me in any way, in the Name of Jesus.

255. Anyone who has targeted me because I rejected them, like the girl I didn't hire because she wasn't a fit for the position, but she shot me the side eye when she left the building-- the Lord Jesus rebuke you, and whatever *spirit* or power that is working in the shootist against me, in the Name of Jesus.

We forget those things that be behind and pressing forward, in the Name of Jesus.

The World Hated Jesus

256.   Lord, anyone who has targeted me because I serve the Only Living God, the Lord Jesus rebuke you, in the Name of Jesus.

If the world hate you, ye know that it hated me before it hated you. (John 15:18)

If I had not done among them the works which none other man did, they had not had sin: but now have they both seen and hated both me and my Father. (John 15:24)

And ye shall be hated of all *men* for my name's sake: but he that endureth to the end shall be saved. (Matthew 10:22, Mark 13:13)

And ye shall
be hated of all *men* for my name's
sake. (Luke 21:17)

257. Anyone who hates me because I
am not worldly—, I'm in it, but not
of it, anyone who has mocked me, let
the Lord rebuke them, in the Name
of Jesus. (John 17:14)

I have given them thy word; and the
world hath hated them, because they
are not of the world, even as I am not
of the world. (John 17:14)

258. Anyone who has targeted me
because I love righteousness and
hate iniquity, the Lord Jesus rebuke
you. (Hebrews 1:9)

259. Lord God when You come You
shall reprove sin, in the Name of
Jesus.

And when he is
come, he will reprove the world of sin,
and of righteousness, and of judgment
(John 16:8)

Thou hast loved righteousness, and
hated iniquity; therefore God, *even* thy
God hath anointed thee with the oil of
gladness above thy fellows.
(Hebrews 1:9)

260.   Lord, in the Name of Jesus, let all
evil strategies, prophecies of
darkness, timetables of hell,
programmed into the heavenlies,
against me--, programmed into the
sun, moon, stars, or in the planets, or
in the dust, or anywhere by the
councils of hell, let them not prevail
against me by those who have
targeted me, in the Name of Jesus.

261.   Let no evil prevail against me,
my body, ministry, life, health,
business, wealth, mind, children,
marriage, spouse, in the Name of
Jesus.

262.   Anyone who has targeted me
because they think I am interested in
their partner or spouse, the Lord

Jesus Christ rebuke you, in the Name of Jesus.

263. Every seed sent by *haters* to cause sickness, disease, pain, poverty in my system be rooted out, and be rendered powerless against me, in the Name of Jesus.

264. Blood of Jesus forbid satanic prayers, and spells, prophecies of darkness. Forbid them, Lord. Do not let them hinder the fulness of life, in the Name of Jesus.

265. I pray to abolish evil words, blood sacrifices, entanglements of iniquity, and all the laws of death, assignments of darkness, programmed by agents of darkness through dust, in the heavenlies, in the Name of Jesus.

266. Anyone who has targeted me, rebuke them, rebuke them, Lord, in the Name of Jesus.

267. I dismantle all evil hexes, vexes, curses, jinxes, and spells from the

minds and mouths of *haters* and all those who target God's people, in the Name of Jesus. Be dismantled now, or return to sender, in the Name of Jesus.

268. Every demonic seed sent by a *hater* that has targeted me to cause sickness, be uprooted now, dry up and wither, in the Name of Jesus.

269. I decree that the Blood of Jesus closes evil portals opened by *haters* of life, in my family, in my bloodline, in the Name of Jesus.

270. Lord, I remove vows of bitterness, vows of pain, vows of darkness, vows of iniquity in this family, in this house, in my blood, and bloodline in the Name of Jesus.

271. I dismiss evil vows of the *haters* who target me for any reason, or no reason at all, in the Name of Jesus.

272. Anyone who has targeted me for no reason at all—just because you just *felt* like it, the Lord Jesus rebuke

you in His hot displeasure, in the
Name of Jesus.

A Hit Out on You?

273.   For those who have been targeted in the spirit, or a hit is out on them in the spirit, may the Lord surround you with His Angels and protection and not even let your foot be dashed on a stone. May the Lord protect you, your going in and your coming out.

- Anyone who is chased in the dream by people
- Anyone who is chased in the dream by animals
- Anyone who is attacked in the dream by animals
- Anyone who is shot at in the dream

- Anyone who has guns pulled on them in the dream
- Anyone in the dream who has been told that they are set for destruction, the Lord Jesus Christ rebuke them.
- Anyone who is the object of hate crimes, either in the spiritual, in the dream, or in the natural
- Anyone suffering through feeding in the dream--

274. Anyone having sex in the dream. The Lord Jesus Christ protect you and deliver you, in the Name of Jesus.

275. The Lord Jesus, by His rebuke **STOPS** the evil powers, and breaks their powers over you, in the Name of Jesus.

276. Lord, stop, these entities, witches, warlocks, wizards scheming their crafts against you, in the Name of Jesus.

277. Lord let the wickedness of the wicked come to an abrupt and permanent end, in the Name of Jesus.

278. Anyone who has targeted me for ritual, the Lord Jesus Christ rebuke you, in the Name of Jesus.

279. Anyone who has targeted me for theft, the Lord render you powerless against me, in the Name of Jesus.

280. Anyone who has targeted me for failure, back to sender, in the Name of Jesus.

281. Anyone who has targeted me for disappointment, or loss, the Lord rebuke you, in the Name of Jesus.

282. Anyone who has targeted me for regret or shame, the Lord Jesus Christ rebuke you, in the Name of Jesus.

Then you will know that I am in Israel, that I am the LORD your God, and that there is no other; never again will my people be shamed. (Joel 2:27)

283.   Anyone who is targeting me with Evil arrows, I AM HIDDEN IN CHRIST, I am hidden UNDER THE SHADOW OF THE ALMIGHTY, so you can't find me, so you miss--, you miss. So, return to sender.

284.   I block you with the shield of faith—every arrow back to sender, back to sender, back to sender, in the Name of Jesus.

285.   Anyone who is targeting me with evil arrows, I MOVE SUDDENLY SO YOU MISS, return to sender, I block you with the shield of faith—every arrow back to sender, in the Name of Jesus.

286.   Anyone who is targeting me with Evil arrows, I send fog and confusion to obscure your eyesight, so you miss, return to sender, I block you with the shield of faith—every arrow back to sender, back to sender, back to sender, in the Name of Jesus.

287. I am not your target. I am not
      your candidate for evil, for harm, or
      hurt. I am not your prey; I shall not
      be devoured, in the Name of Jesus
      (Ezekiel 34:28)

They shall no more be a prey to the
nations, nor shall the beasts of the land
devour them, they shall dwell securely,
and none shall make them afraid.
(Ezekiel 23:18 ESV)

288. Anyone targeting me for evil
      exchange, I reverse any exchange
      you've done on me, my life, my
      health, my ministry, my spouse, my
      family, my children, my destiny, in
      the Name of Jesus.

289. Anyone targeting me for evil
      load, I reject your evil load, take it
      back, you carry your own load, in the
      Name of Jesus.

290. Anyone targeting me to send any
      evil thing, or any evil condition into
      my life, I reject what you are sending
      and command it to ricochet back to

you; failed assignment, in the Name of Jesus.

291.   Any strongman sitting on me, my life, my lap or any part of me or my destiny, the Lord Jesus rebuke you and the mighty Angels of God bind you and take you away, in the Name of Jesus.

292.   All users, takers, haters, the Lord rebuke you. Take your evil plans and leave my life immediately and permanently, in the Name of Jesus.

For in him we live, and move, and have our being; as certain also of your own poets have said, For we are also his offspring.

Forasmuch then as we are the offspring of God, we ought not to think that the Godhead is like unto gold, or silver, or stone, graven by art and man's device.

And the times of this ignorance God winked at; but now commandeth all men every where to repent:

Because he hath appointed a day, in the which he will judge the world in righteousness by that man whom he hath ordained; whereof he hath given assurance unto all men, in that he hath raised him from the dead. (Acts 17:28-31)

293. I seal these words, decrees, declarations and prayers across every dimension, age, era, epoch, timeline, past, present, and future, to infinity. I seal them with the Blood of Jesus and the Holy Spirit of Promise, in the Name of Jesus.

294. Any retaliation against the speaker, listener, or anyone praying or will ever pray these prayers, decrees and declarations in the future – Lord let that retaliation be rendered null and void and return with Fire on the head of the perpetrator without Mercy and to infinity, in the Name of Jesus.

Amen. *Thank You, Lord. Hallelujah!*

Dear Reader

Thank you for acquiring and reading this book. Thank you for supporting this ministry.

May the Lord surround you as with a shield and keep you from all harm, harassment and danger from anyone who may have targeted you for any reason, in the Name of Jesus.

If this book has blessed you, please leave a review or comment on the platform where you purchased it. That simple act causes more people to see the book on that platform.

Shalom,

Dr. Marlene Miles

Prayerbooks by this author

While most books by this author have prayer points either throughout the book or at the end, there are some books that are only prayers. You just open up the book and pray.

Prayers Against Barrenness: *For Success in Business and Life*

Fruit of the Womb: *Prayers Against Barrenness*

Beauty Curses, *Warfare Prayers Against* https://a.co/d/5Xlc20M

Courts of Marriage: Prayers for Marriage in the Courts of Heaven
(prayerbook) https://a.co/d/cNAdgAq

Courtroom Warfare @ Midnight
(prayerbook) https://a.co/d/5fc7Qdp

Demonic Cobwebs *(prayerbook)*
https://a.co/d/fp9Oa2H

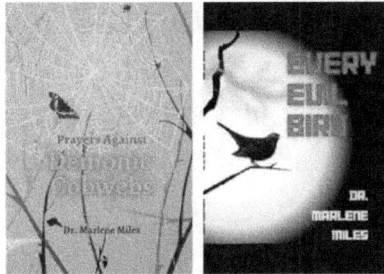

Every Evil Bird https://a.co/d/hF1kh1O

Gates of Thanksgiving

I AM NOT YOUR TARGET: *Warfare Against Haters & the Powers They Employ*

Spirits of Death, Hell & the Grave, Pass Over Me and My House

Throne of Grace: Courtroom Prayer

Warfare Prayer Against Poverty
https://a.co/d/bZ61lYu

Other books by this author

AK: The Adventures of the Agape Kid

Already Married in the Spirit: *Why You May Not Be Married in the Natural*

AMONG SOME THIEVES
https://a.co/d/dkYT4ZV

Ancestral Powers

Anti-Marriage, *The Spirit of*

Backstabbers https://a.co/d/gi8iBxf

Barrenness, *Prayers Against*
https://a.co/d/feUltIs

Battlefield of Marriage, *The*

Beware of the Dog: Prayers Against Dogs in the Dream.

Bless Your Food: *Let the Dining Table be Undefiled*

Blindsided: *Has the Old Man Bewitched You?* https://a.co/d/5O2fLLR

Break Free from Collective Captivity

Broken Spirits & Dry Bones

By Means of a Whorish Father

Casting Down Imaginations

Churchzilla, The Wanna-Be,
Supposed-to-be Bride of Christ

Demonic Cobwebs (prayerbook)

Demonic Time Bombs

Demons Hate Questions

Devil Loves Trauma, *The*

Devil Weapons: Unforgiveness,
Bitterness,...

The Devourers: Thieves of Darkness 2

Do Not Swear by the Moon

Don't Refuse Me, Lord (4 book series)
https://a.co/d/idP34LG

Dream Defilement

The Emptiers: *Thieves of Darkness, 1*
https://a.co/d/5I4n5mc

Evil Touch

Failed Assignment

Fantasy Spirit Spouse
https://a.co/d/hW7oYbX

FAT Demons (The): *Breaking Demonic Curses* https://a.co/d/4kP8wV1

The Fold (5-book series)

- The Fold (Book 1)
- Name Your Seed (Book 2)
- The Poor Attitudes of Money (3)
- Do Not Orphan Your Seed (4)
- For the Sake of the Gospel (5)
- My Sowing Journal

Gang Ups: Touch Not God's Anointed

Getting Rid of Evil Spiritual Food

https://a.co/d/i2L3WYQ

got HEALING? Verses for Life

got LOVE? Verses for Life

got HOPE? Verses for Life

got money? https://a.co/d/g2av41N

Here Come the Horns: *Skilled to Destroy*
https://a.co/d/cZiNnkP

Hidden Sins: Hidden Iniquity

https://a.co/d/4Mth0wa

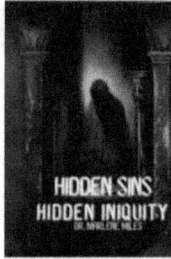

How to Dental Assist

How to Dental Assist2: Be Productive, Not Wasteful

How to STOP Being a Blind Witch or Warlock

I AM NOT YOUR TARGET: *Warfare Against Haters and the Powers they Employ*

I Take It Back

Legacy

Let Me Have A Dollar's Worth
https://a.co/d/h8F8XgE

Level the Playing Field

Living for the NOW of God

Lose My Location
https://a.co/d/crD6mV9

Love Breaks Your Heart

Made Perfect In Love

Mammon https://a.co/d/29yhMG7

Man Safari, *The*

Marriage Ed. Rules of Engagement & Marriage

Made Perfect in Love

Money Hunters: Beware of Those

Money on the Altar https://a.co/d/4EqJ2Nr

Mulberry Tree, *The*
https://a.co/d/9nR9rRb

Motherboard (The) ~ *Soul Prosperity Series*

Name Your Seed

Occupy: *Until I Return*
https://a.co/d/bZ7ztUy

Plantation Souls

Players Gonna Play

Portals: Shut the Front Door: Prayers to
Close Evil Portals.

Power Money: Nine Times the Tithe

https://a.co/d/gRt41gy

The Power to Get Wealth
https://a.co/d/e4ub4Ov

Powers Above

The Robe, Part 1, The Lessons of Joseph

The Robe, Part II, The Lessons of Joseph

Seasons of Grief

Seasons of Waiting

Seasons of War

Second Marriage, Third--, *Any Marriage*

https://a.co/d/6m6GN4N

Seducing Spirits: Idolatry & Whoredoms

https://a.co/d/4Jq4WEs

Shut the Front Door: *Prayers to Close Portals* https://a.co/d/cH4TWJj

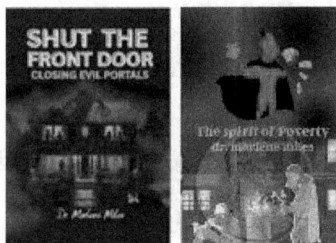

Sift You Like Wheat

Six Men Short: What Has Happened to all the Men?

SLAVE

Soul Prosperity soul prosperity series 3

https://a.co/d/5p8YvCN

Souls Captivity soul prosperity series 2

The Spirit of Anti-Marriage

The Spirit of Poverty
https://a.co/d/abV2o2e

Spiritual Thieves
https://a.co/d/eqPPz33

StarStruck~ Triangular Power series.

SUNBLOCK~ Triangular Power series.

The Swallowers: *Thieves of Darkness,* 3

Take It Back

This Is NOT That: How to Keep
Demons from Coming at You

Time Is of the Essence

Too Many Wives: *Why You Have Lady
Problems*

Tormenting Spirits
https://a.co/d/dAogEJf

Toxic Souls

Triangular Power *(series)*

- Powers Above
- SUNBLOCK
- Do Not Swear by the Moon
- STARSTRUCK

Unbreak My Heart: *Don't Let Me Die*

Uncontested Doom

Unguarded Hours, *The*

Unseen Life, *The* (forthcoming)

Upgrade: How to Get Out of Survival Mode

- Toxic Souls (Book 2 of series)
- Legacy (Book 3 of series)

The Wasters: *Thieves of Darkness,* Bk 2
https://a.co/d/bUvI9Jo

What Have You to Declare? What Do You Have With You from Where You've Been?

When I Was A Child, *I Prayed As a Child*

When the Devourer is Rebuked

https://a.co/d/1HVv8oq

The Wilderness Romance *(series)* This series is about conducting a Godly relationship and marriage with someone who is a Wilderness person. It is about how to recognize it and navigate through it. These books are about how not to get caught up in such.

- *The Social Wilderness*
- *The Sexual Wilderness*
- *The Spiritual Wilderness*

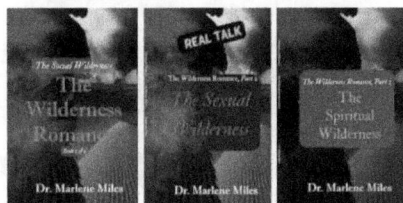

Other Series

The Fold (a series on Godly finances)
https://a.co/d/4hz3unj

Soul   Prosperity   Series

https://a.co/d/bz2M42q

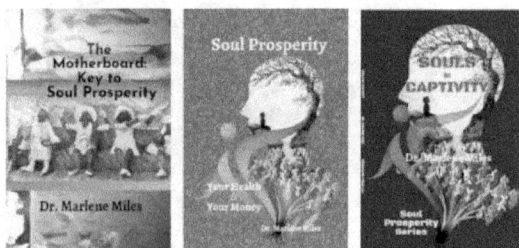

Spirit Spouse books

https://a.co/d/9VehDSo

https://a.co/d/97sKOwm

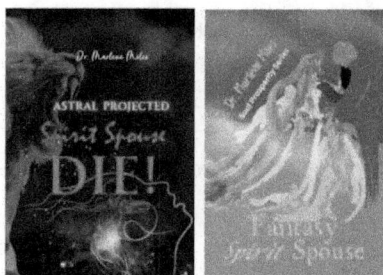

Battlefield of Marriage, The

https://a.co/d/eUDzizO

Players Gonna Play

https://a.co/d/2hzGw3N

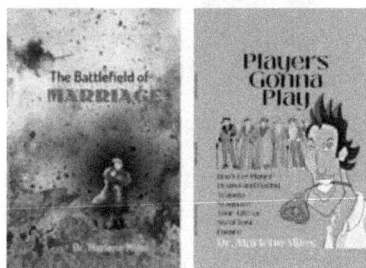

Sent Spirit Spouse (can someone send you a spirit spouse? This book is not yet released.)

Matters of the Heart

Made Perfect in Love
https://a.co/d/70MQW3O

Love Breaks Your Heart
https://a.co/d/4KvuQLZ

Unbreak My Heart
https://a.co/d/84ceZ6M

Broken Spirits & Dry Bones
https://a.co/d/e6iedNP

Thieves of Darkness series

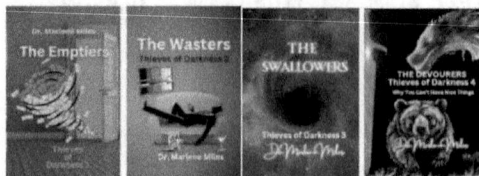

The Emptiers https://a.co/d/heio0dO

The Wasters https://a.co/d/5TG1iNQ

The Swallowers
https://a.co/d/1jWhM6G

The Devourers: Why We Can't Have Nice
Things https://a.co/d/87Tejbf

Spiritual Thieves

Triangular Powers https://a.co/d/aUCjAWC

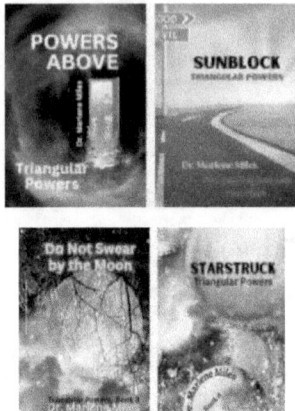

Upgrade (series) *How to Get Out of Survival Mode* https://a.co/d/aTERhX0